Dreams
What Are They & What Do They Mean

Lady Mary Hatter

© Copyright 2021, Lady Mary Hatter

All Rights Reserved.

In accordance with the U.S. Copyright Act of 1976, the scanning, uploading, and electronic sharing of any part of this book without the permission of the publisher constitute unlawful privacy and theft of the author's intellectual property. If you would like to use material from the book (other than for preview purposes), prior written permission must be obtained by contacting the publisher at the address below. Thank you for your support of the author's rights.

ISBN: 978-1-60414-292-1

Visit the author's website for more information:

www.MaryHatter.com

See your dreams come to life with D.I.S.H.!

Divine

Interpretations

Spiritually

Heard!

Table of Contents

Introduction vii

Dreams and Interpretations 1

Conclusion 65

About the Author 69

Introduction

I'm so amazed! I'm so excited! God has done it again! He has blessed me, to be a blessing! I received a word from God on September 16, 2016, that I'm a "Dream Interpreter!" When He spoke this, I just told Him, "I receive."

Let's look at some definitions of dreams.

1. A series of thoughts, images, or emotions occurring during sleep.
2. A strongly desired goal or purpose.

God reminded me of how, for years people came to me and told me what they dreamed about and they asked if I knew what their dreams meant. I would tell them what I thought they meant, not knowing then, but I know now, that it was God is giving me the interpretation to give them. On September 16, 2016, God revealed to me, that I was a Dream Interpreter. He's given me another gift to bless and help the body of Christ and the world. He explained to me, that I was to write down the dream, mediate on it, and listen to Holy Spirit as he gives me the interpretation of the dream. This is the order from God!

You will notice there are some dreams with the dates listed, they are the ones that's most important: as we know they all are important; however, God wants more attention on these.

Dreams can be good and sometimes seem bad to us; however, God given dreams are meant for our good, because He's all good. "The dreams we think are bad, are to help fix the problems we are having in our soul;" says Apostle Dr. Leroy Thompson.

On this day of October 12, 2016, God began to layout the format of this book that He's given me to write. I'm to write down the dream first, and then write down the interpretation that Holy Spirit has revealed to me from Him. On last night while I was dreaming God spoke these words to me. **"STRAP."** In this dream, I was writing down these words, and then I woke up. I asked God what the letters meant and He told me:

STRAP
Spirit
Trust
Receive
Anointed
Purpose

I began to work the process like God explained above. I only remember and retain what God wants me to take away from the dreams. They're not just for myself however, others also. Even though I didn't understand the dream at first, I relied on

D.I.S.H.
Divine
Interpretations
Spiritually
Heard

by way of Holy Spirit. I follow Gods plans. I hear only what His Spirit speaks, and the revelations come and remain, as His people reign. I walk in the **Spirit**. I **Trust** God. I **Receive**. I'm **Anointed**. I walk in my **Purpose**. I'm anointed to prosper. These words came about as I mediated and listened to the Holy Ghost. Look at this scripture, God explains it this way:

> Then the LORD said to me, "Write my answer plainly on tablets, so that a runner can carry the correct message to others. This vision is for a future time. It describes the end, and it will be fulfilled. If it seems slow in coming, wait patiently, for it will surely take place. It will not be delayed."
>
> **Habakkuk 2:2-3 NLT**

God wants us to understand and know what our dreams mean. He wants us to receive all that comes from Him. God has given me dreams and interpretations of dreams, for myself and others. All for His glory. He receives the glory, not I. I receive, and you must receive the supernatural surplus, that He's given us. What I see, and have seen, I thank God for giving it all to me. I explain the dreams just as He gave me the interpretation of them.

I know you will rejoice, and be exceedingly glad; to know what God has given, and continue to give, is better than you have ever had. Take to heart what God has placed in our hearts.

Before writing this book, I had this dream of someone giving me money: and I passed the money to my husband. God showed me in this dream that I'm to share in my marriage first, and then share with others who He tells me to bless.

I'm grateful to God for trusting and using me to get His word out in other ways, so that we all receive our blessings. He allowed me to speak what He revealed to me in my book, *Things Seen In The Spirit*, and now I'm interpreting the dreams that He wants fulfilled in our lives. I'm encouraged, and I know that you will be too, if you *read on*.

Let's see what God has in store. *See yourself there.* This place of peace, protection, provisions, promises, promotions, power, and prosperity. All because God has pleasure in the prosperity of His people.

Blessings always!

October 22, 2016

Dream

My husband took me to another city to shop. I was shopping for Michael Kors pants. The lady in the store was trying to get me to accept less quality and thought that I couldn't afford the real quality clothes. She was telling me the highest price for the pants, as if I would say forget them. I continued shopping until I found the ones I wanted. Another sales associate started helping me. This was a male. He begin to bring all different types and styles of pants. Price wasn't a problem. I left the store with styles I've never seen before.

Interpretation

Increase. God is giving me the desires of my heart. I can go where I want to go and shop. I'm Gods best and I receive His best. The best of everything, and more of everything. People will try and talk me out of what God has given me. There will always be someone that will honor and respect me for who I am and give me what I desire, no matter the price. I have unlimited cash flow.

God has allowed the people to see and cater to me. I'm His own, because of the seeds I've sown.

October 22, 2016

Dream

I was on a cruise. A large ship and large body of water with no ending. People were swimming and having a good time. I begin to observe the people in the water and their activities; then I started to give the captain ideas and suggestions for making the cruise better. He listened to me and started changing things immediately. Some people was following me and asking me questions. I sent them to the captain for further instructions. I knew that I wasn't in charge however to assist the captain. He knew that I was there to help him. I stayed in my place and enjoyed the cruise.

Interpretation

I'm receiving, enjoying and living the best in life. The never-ending waters represents the throne of grace; which is Gods never ending power. I have the wisdom, knowledge, understanding and power of God, that He's given me. Even though I have the power to hear, listen and do, I never take over who has been placed in charge over me. I walk in the supernatural. People of God recognize the anointing on me. This scripture explains:

> He is the Holy Spirit, who leads into all truth.
> The world cannot receive him, because it isn't looking for him and doesn't recognize him.

> But you know him, because he lives with you now and later will be in you.
>
> **John 14:17 NLT**

When I obey God, people and things change for the good because of my presence and the anointing that's been given me from God. I know what, when, where, and how to receive from Him; and life is good and we enjoy!

> And we know that God causes everything to work together for the good of those who love God and are called according to his purpose for them.
>
> **Romans 8:28 NLT**

October 27, 2016

Dream

In this dream Pastor Briggs took my husband and I out to dinner. Before we got on the elevator he asked me to put his shoes on my feet and I proceeded to do so. No questions asked. I said to him that his shoes fit my feet perfectly, which was strange that his shoes fitted. After dinner he said he had to go to his mother's house. We never actually went to her house or even meet his mother. He brought us back home. I then went into another part of this dream; Bishop Jones, Pastor Brenda Jones, my husband and I were all lying in our bed, and I said this bed is big enough for us all to fit. We all agreed. Next, I had a large nice pen in my hand and Bishop Jones asked me for it and I gave it to him with no problem. I just figured he wanted mine because it was nicer looking and bigger. I just used another plain looking, and smaller one. That was the end of the dream.

Interpretation

We have been elevated to higher levels. We are wearing and walking in wealth. We have the same self-anointing. Kindred spirits. God is no respecter of persons, what He's done for one in principle, He's done the same in principle for us. Gods Pastor's and prophets are feeding, nurturing, loving, and giving to us. His pastors and prophets are by our side. They are comfortable with us and they trust us. They will use us in ministry, because God has spoken to them to do so. Bishop asking for my pen was to show me where I was with God and to obey Him and by giving to the prophet we receive what God has already prepared and promised us to prosper. We must believe His prophets so shall we prosper.

November 20, 2016

Dream
Tange Dream

She was in Chicago at my mother-in-law's house. People she recognized in the house were, my mother-in-law, and myself. There were others but she didn't recognize their faces. I was sitting at the table in the kitchen, however, I didn't say anything. Others were talking about this cat, that was dangerous and not to let it in. Tange was wondering why a cat was dangerous, however she did as they said. She went through the house and closed all the windows. However, when she returned to the kitchen where I was sitting, she saw the cat had gotten into the house. She began to love on the cat, by stroking its fur, hugging and kissing it. She noticed the cat wasn't dangerous as people said. She told them and they saw that the cat wasn't dangerous as they believed it was. This is the message of the dream. See below:

Interpretation

Even in familiar places, people could miss the message God is speaking to them; if they are not tapped into the spirit realm. The person sitting there that's tapped in had to sit by quietly, so the others could receive the message. People perceived that it was dangerous instead of recognizing that it was love trying to make its presence known in their house.

The person that shows love listened to the ones that didn't know it was the message from God, as they tried to shut love out, not knowing. Love found its way in the house without them knowing. Once love found its way in, the person with the compassion had to hear and demonstrate the love, to show the real truth of the matter, that, instead of the danger they believed it to be, was only Gods message of love.

This person with compassion had to learn, that even though others are believing and saying things; she had to know for herself, because people will miss God and she will be listening to the wrong thing, by listening to people that didn't know what His message was. It's always good to know what God is saying, obey and receive it for yourself.

December 31, 2016

Dream

In this dream my sister-in-law Dana was talking to me. She was saying mean and evil things to and about me. As she was talking I saw my husband just standing there not saying or telling her to stop talking to me this way. He just looked and listened in silence. I listened, and then begin to tell her to read **2 Timothy 2:16.** I reminded her of what I told her years ago, that she was called to preach.

After I walked away from her, there was a young man sitting by observing also. He was quoting scriptures. I asked him if he was a pastor? He answered, "you can say that?" So, I took that as a yes. We all begin to walk away. I told Dana she needs to get herself together. She said, "I know because I have people that would follow me." I woke up with this scripture in my head. I looked it up, and read what it said. Let's read it.

> Avoid worthless, foolish talk that only leads to more godless behavior.
>
> **2 Timothy 2:16 NLT**

Interpretation

God wants me to know that I'm His approved worker. I can't entertain foolish behavior. I must know what to say and how to answer. God's truth stands firm like a foundation stone. The Lord knows those who are His, and all who belong to Him must turn away from evil. I must walk away from anything that people allow the enemy to use. Instead, I must pursue righteous living, faithfulness, love, and peace. Enjoy the companionship of those who call on the Lord with pure hearts.

Don't get upset with my husband for not saying anything, and the young man sitting observing, which was quoting scriptures. I didn't need rescuing from the situation, however — I handled it the way God would have me to. I listened, and spoke what God said.

Again, never get involved in foolish, ignorant arguments that only start fights. I'm a servant of the Lord, and I must not quarrel, but be kind to everyone, be able to teach, and be patient with difficult people. I must gently instruct those who oppose the truth.

I must pray that people will want God to change their hearts, and they will learn the truth. Then they will come to their senses and escape from the devil's trap. For they have been held captive by him to do whatever he wants. God also showed me the scripture of what He spoke to me for 2017. He said, *"Staying Clean and Receiving Everything in 2017."*

Here's the scripture. Let's read it.

> If you keep yourself pure, you will be a special utensil for honorable use. Your life will be clean, and you will be ready for the Master to use you for every good work.
>
> **2 Timothy 2:21 NLT**

Dream

This dream started out with my sister, Juanita and her son Damien. We were all on a cruise to what looked like Africa. The people looked like they were from Africa. They were drawn to me, as I talked with them, and they tried to get me to buy things from them and showed me how to be safe while on my cruise.

As the dream continued, I saw a friend of mine (Bell) from over 15 years ago — it's been that long since I last spoke with her. I saw my mom in this dream also. We were stopped at one of the locations the ship was docked at for the cruise.

As we preceded back on the ship, we all went separate directions. I tried different areas of the ship looking for Juanita and Damien. It took me awhile, and I finally saw Juanita coming out of her room. I explained that I was trying for an hour trying to locate them.

She was dressed and headed to eat. I asked where her son was, she replied, "I don't know."

I told her, "I'm going to get dressed and we will get something to eat."

We continued on and preceded to get something to eat. I never saw Damien after that. End of dream.

Interpretation

My sister, nephew and I was doing fun and happy things together, and got off track. My friend and mom |

will always be their with us, however they aren't physically there. These are people we love dearly. This is the display of love that family should cherish. Juanita was once in a fun happy place. Now she's indecisive as to where to go, however she's willing to make the necessary steps to go.

Damien on the other hand might not be willing or ready to go at this time. As I searched for him, he wasn't anywhere to be found. Juanita and I were determined to go without him.

Regardless of what people do we have to continue to do what God has placed, and positioned for us to do. We must purpose in our hearts to finish what we start.

Walking with God isn't always an easy task; however, we must continue to keep pressing, pushing, and forget about the past. We have to go with the goers.

Juanita was temporarily unreachable, but was found. Juanita had to stop waiting and depending on her children, and live on.

Eating is food for the body, but hearing God is being spiritually-minded and having peace, despite the circumstances and situations around you. They both bring satisfaction and substance to serve the soul.

When we continue on living for God we receive blessings untold, as they continue to unfold. Never let no one or nothing stop you from doing what God told you to do.

February 17, 2017

Dream

I was in this huge banquet hall which sat over a huge body of water, and it looked as if there wasn't an ending to this huge body of water. The place had lots of people. The first group of African-American people I interacted with were playing old school music and no one was dancing.

I looked around and said to myself, "This isn't where I want to be," and immediately, I moved away from that group.

I came across another group of European people that were dressed in formal wear. Everything was elegant. I said, "This fits," and I joined in with them. People were socializing, being friendly and getting to know each other.

As time passed, this huge banquet hall began to rise higher and higher, and I said, "I didn't know this was a ship." I was at the front of the banquet hall as it went higher and higher. It had glass around it, and I could see outside as it rose up, and there was the water right below.

I made sure I wasn't at the edge of the glass as it began to start moving forward. I rose up, then moved forward, came back down, and landed perfectly back on the water. No one was afraid. It was as if it was supposed to happen this way.

I stepped out onto another level of this hall, as one lady held my hand and assisted me. I was walking down what I thought was a hallway, but it looked like a runway.

At the end of it was this huge body of water, with no way to cross and no dry land in sight.

I went back to the banquet hall, and finished socializing with the same group of people. As time passed, I left because there was suddenly land on the other side of this huge body of water.

I had a great time. However, after I left this banquet hall, I saw people from my past but didn't interact with them because as soon as I noticed them, immediately they were gone. This was the end of the dream.

Interpretation

God has elevated me to higher heights and deeper depths. A land of no scarceness, never ending and the supernatural. I have moved away from the people and things that wasn't progressing and old ways, and I've moved into a place and people of newness and prosperity.

I recognized the past, however but didn't go back to it or the people. Now that God has taken me to new levels in Christ Jesus, I don't desire to, and will not return to the things of old. I shall continue to walk in, live in, and receive supernatural blessings as they never cease to unfold.

Higher heights deeper depths, I have gone beyond, and all my needs have been met. I have moved into supernatural supply, I'm sustaining, multiplying, and all my fruits are remaining. Fruits of my lips and labor. I receive my new and higher levels. I have power over devils.

March 4, 2017

Dream

I was walking with a group of women following behind me. Everyone was following and they were gathered in a crowd from all sides but no one got in front of me. As I turned around and looked at the women following, I saw one lady raise her foot as if she was trying to kick me in the back. I just looked at her saw who she was, and she looked back at me, and put her foot back down. The others in crowd following grabbed ahold of her after she put her foot down. She was removed from the crowd and we preceded to walk forward.

Interpretation

I will be leading women and they will follow along. Everyone following won't be with you. God will allow them to follow to reveal and expose who they really are. You have His Holy Ghost power and authority to stare down the enemy and he will obey you, and flee. He can't hurt you. God's angels are always protecting you.

He will allow others to help you that want to be led properly and follow properly. God allows others to assist and help get rid of the dead weight that's following. The work must and shall continue on. Nothing and no one can stop the work or walk, because it's according to God's will that we prosper, as we are His workmanship created in Christ Jesus to do good works, and it's already been ordained by God.

> For we are his workmanship, created in Christ Jesus unto good works, which God hath before ordained that we should walk in them.
>
> **Ephesians 2:10 KJV.**

March 11, 2017

Dream

I was in a large important church service, with lots of people. Pastor James and Pastor Teresa White was there. Pastor Melvin Lewis Sr. was there also. He was looking on from the side, amazed at what was happening and that we were there.

My husband told me to bless Pastor Lewis with $20. I did just that. During the service someone shouted out, "The broke Hatters!" I wasn't able to see that person's face.

My husband told me to bless that person with money. I asked why, and he said because he or she just talked about us. I thought my husband just wanted to give the person money to show him or her that we did, in fact, have money.

Interpretation

God has elevated us to higher levels in Christ Jesus. The people that others see as prosperous isn't as high as people think they are. We were a part of this large, important service and people will see where God has taken us.

My husband saying bless that person with money, meant that we are to bless and pray for those who misuse or say evil against us. People will be jealous of our elevation and say things that they don't know. They want to make others think like them. They are blinded by envious and jealousy.

Because of our teachings, training, and obedience to sow seeds; the harvest has come, and victory over lack and not enough, we have won. God has given this to His very elect ones. I receive.

> What joy for the nation whose God is the LORD, whose people he has chosen as his inheritance.
>
> **Psalms 33:12 NLT**

March 15, 2017

Dream

We was at Dr. Moore and his wife's house. This was a large house with decorated iron gates around it. A small section of gates on one side and a tall section in the main entrance. Pastor and I was talking to Dr. Moore then we left and went to a church service, where pastor walked up with his assistant named Stephen. He introduced him to Dr. Moore, then pastor and I walked away.

Dr. Moore didn't say anything to pastor in front of his assistant, he just walked away and waited to speak to pastor and I alone. He told pastor that this man was not a good person to assist him, and that he needed to remove him.

After Dr. Moore walked away, pastor said, "I'm gonna keep Stephen because I liked how he assisted me, and Dr. Moore was wrong about him."

Dr. Moore and I began talking, and he said that my husband needed to trust God and him about what he said regarding Stephen, and know that he hears from God.

I listened, and said, "I know he will hear God and do what's right."

He said okay and asked how I was doing. I told him I was great, and I began to share about my books. I talked more about my newest release, The Secrets Are Out, and he congratulated me on my success.

In the next part of the dream: I went into the kitchen where Lady Moore was preparing a meal. After that, we went outside in the front of the house where the beautiful black decorated gates were.

On one side was a smaller gate and the center was the main entrance with the tall larger gate, as I mentioned earlier. Lady Moore closed and locked the smaller gate and went back inside the house.

I noticed a poor homeless guy come up to the large gate and I walked over to the gate and locked it, so the man couldn't come in. Soon after that, detectives came up to the gate and said they had been watching this man for some time, and they asked permission to enter through the gate so they could arrest him."

Next, I encountered men with guns, and I didn't fear them, I just stared at them and knew that they would be captured, so I walked away. When I looked around, I saw

Lady Mary Hatter

that this Stephen, my husband's assistant, was in fact the man that the detectives had been looking for. Stephen and the guys with guns were all arrested.

I went back into the house, and as I entered the kitchen, there was Lady Moore finishing up the meal, while Dr. Moore and my husband were having a conversation. Dr. Moore was ministering and giving him wisdom. He embraced us as brothers and sisters. End of dream.

Interpretation

My husband has to listen to wisdom as God gives him wise counsel.

> "My son, pay attention to my wisdom; listen carefully to my wise counsel."
>
> **Proverbs 5:1 NLT**

Regardless of what pastor thought he knew, or what he thinks a person can do for him, he should hear who God has given wisdom to speak to him for his good. God knows best, and he uses his people to help us, because we are chosen to excel far greater than the rest.

When I locked the gate on the poor man, God was saying that poverty has to stay out, and it can never come back again. Encountering guys with guns, or my enemies; as I stared them down, this meant, I wasn't afraid of them. I had to recognize and see Stephen, so that I could witness what God had spoken to Dr. Moore about him.

He was exposed and arrested with the others. God had already revealed him to Dr. Moore. Pastor on the other hand, has to listen to wisdom and respect wise counsel from God's chosen man. God allowed Dr. Moore to minister to him.

May 3, 2017

Dream

I was in a Church service, not sure what type of service it was; while in this service I stepped out to go to the lady's room. In the lady's room, there was First Lady Pamela Dimes and another lady I didn't recognize. They were just sitting in there talking. There was only two stalls and one was nasty. I used the cleaner one, and afterwards Lady Pamela began to explain to me about wearing tight girdles. I listened to her and thanked her and walked out.

The next part of this dream, there was a young lady that wanted to testify of what the church had done for her. I then recognized it was the new church my husband and I were leaders of. (Pastor and First Lady) This lady testified of how the church had helped her to come out of her bad situations, and now she lives for God wholeheartedly.

Others began testifying also. As they were testifying I was up front, and when they finished, I began prophesying and people received. I prayed and service was over. At the end of service, I left out and there was Pastor Brenda Jones, saying help her with her dress, she has to speak at the next service. I helped her and dream was over.

Interpretation

In this dream, God showed me that I can't just sit down on my gifts. I must prophesy of what God wants His people to know. They will have life changing experiences to testify of, and build up His kingdom. I can't stay in the company of people who aren't doing the work for God, and just want to promote their own agendas at this time. I have to respect and love them for where they're at right now. There's lots of work to be done.

People who are willing, and obedient are the ones that want to live a changed life walking according to God's purpose for them. People will appreciate the work pastor and I are doing and testify of God's goodness. God has allowed us to lead a new group of people that's ready and willing to give their lives wholeheartedly to Him, and help get His work done. Pastor Brenda will work with us in spreading the gospel of Jesus Christ, and we will work closely together in advancing God's Kingdom.

Dream

I was entering a room where there were some of my family members. There was my Aunt Flora Dunn (Ann), Great Aunt Aliene, Cousin Wendy, Brother John L., and lots of other cousins. My brother John L. asked one of my male cousins if he could find guns in this particular space, and he said yes and did so. I looked at the guns, but didn't say anything to them or even let them know I had seen the guns at that time.

We went into another room, where lots of other family members were present. In this room, I began prophesying, and all my family listened quietly and the male cousins that found and showed the guns to my brother John L., they listened closely as he stared at me. He gave his life to God and immediately started praying.

My other family members saw him change, and they began to pray and weep. We had an awesome time, and I prayed for everyone, and that part of dream was over. The next part of dream there was a European American man, and the late Pastor Dr. Kenneth Skelton. Pastor Skelton told this man he would do intercessory prayer before service on Sundays. I thought to myself why? Because he didn't see him do anything. I didn't question him about this. Dream was over.

Interpretation

When I obey God, even the people in my family that I've seen doing wrong can change. I must be still, don't move or speak to quick, especially on my own, wait on Gods instructions, hear, listen, and do; when and as He tells me to. Speak His Word, in season and out of season: when they want to hear, and when they don't want to hear. Never be afraid to speak what God has said, and shall continue to say, through His Holy Spirit to me.

There had to be a coming together of family members to see the goodness of God, and they had to see the ones that were once not living for Him, change, and know that since He did it for one, He can do the same for them also.

If we can't help our own family, how are we going to help others? Charity starts at home, and then spreads abroad.

Pastor Skelton represented, not to question authority who has a proven record, or someone you know that has lived their life for God. *Why?* I wondered. But didn't question him. As God showed Pastor Skelton He will allow Pastor AD and I to know who should be in leadership and help with kingdom work. God uses His examples in the earth and in heaven. Praise God!

Dream

I was at another hairstylist, my original one wasn't available to do my hair. My husband dropped me off there, paid and left. When I finished up, I was trying to reach him to pick me up. He was unreachable, and never showed back up to take me home.

I left the location, and encountered men that was trying to harm me. Each corner I turned more of them appeared trying to attack me. I raised my hands and all of a sudden, I had two long sharp instruments in both hands to fight with. I used them to attack these men, and I got away.

The next part to dream, I was driving a car along with two of my sisters, Diane and Juanita, and the young woman who styled my hair. I was taking her home. She told me of a sick relative that was staying at her house. I asked her to put this sick family member in the car with us. She did just that, and we proceeded to church.

As the dream continues, we were in church, and I saw that the sick lady, and the hairstylist were laying on a cot all covered up. While God's Word was being taught, the lady started moving and uncovered herself. Then she was in the pulpit, telling her testimony of how she was healed.

Next part of service was the offering. Myself and my sister Diane were asked to give a hundred dollars, and we did so. Then, I was in another church service, with my friend Elaine. She, and her husband (Reggie) were assistants to the pastor and his wife.

She said she felt God wanted the pastor and church to hear what I had in me from Him. I explained how she should approach her pastor with what she felt God led her to say about me. That was the end of the dream.

Interpretation

I was outside of my normal routine. My husband wasn't there, and couldn't help me go through what I had to encounter or do. Even through the enemies tried to harm me, they were defeated. The weapons will be formed against me, but they will not prosper. God supernaturally equipped me with the tools to use, as He gave me a way of escape. I was delivered from the hands of the enemy; however, I had to do something with what He had given me. I wasn't afraid and just kept moving, and God stepped in to deliver me.

While being outside of my comfort zone, I wasn't fearful of the enemy, I obeyed, and did what God allowed me to do. Because of my obedience, people were healed, and testimonies came forth immediately.

The Kingdom of God was blessed also from the offerings. Seeds should be sown, not just because we need money, but for other things like healing and deliverance also.

Lastly God uses others to hear Him and continue the process, promotions, and prosperity, of His work being done in His Kingdom. We must hear, listen and obey Him, at all times, at all cost. Never fear because He is always near.

May 13, 2017

Dream

In this dream; I was at work, talking with a young lady about the bad things going on in this world. She was one of my coworkers. I was also telling her about Mrs. Cytitia Jones (my hairstylist). I said that she would join us later, because she always knows or have some input on things, or what to do.

Later on, she came and joined us in the discussion. We all were discussing what or how we could help people receive Jesus Christ and live wholeheartedly for God. Our desire is for people to live the abundant life in Christ. Our main focus was that we would witness to people and invite them to church. We were saying that our witness is how we live in our everyday lives. I invited the two of them to my church.

The next part of the dream; we were inside this huge Church. This was a huge building with lots of open space, like a warehouse. My husband and I were the Pastors of this Church. We were in morning worship and the young people was doing praise and worship. Lots of young people began to come in the church and began joining in with the singing.

When they finished, I began asking visitors who invited them. They were saying the people that invited them were the ones I had invited to come to church. As I invited people to come, they were inviting others to come to our church.

They enjoyed the young people singing. They were happy about how we had young people praising and worshiping God. In others words, they were drawn by the young people. The young and old were drawn.

We began to welcome each other as though no one was a visitor, just all being happy to see each other again. The young people continued singing, worshipping and praising God, with loud voices, shouting, raising their hands, giving Him the glory.

Massive amounts of people continued to come into the church as fellowshipping was going on. People were crying tears of joy as welcoming of the visitors were continuing. People began to ask how they could be a part of our church. This was an awesome experience. People being saved and joining our church as we were welcoming the visitors. End of dream.

Interpretation

We were at work, not a physical job, but for God. I have people around me that's serious about bringing souls into the kingdom and helping me to do so. There are people that I know, and others that I don't know of right now, but they're all ready and willing to help me. I must be willing and ready to witness at all times, to bring souls into The Kingdom of God.

God will give us the huge space, to house the massive amounts of people, that are ready to give their lives to Him. The young people will and are being used like never before! They have a desire for God, as they were singing, worshiping and praising God: in doing so, they invoked the presence of God, and inspired the people.

The unsaved will be led to Christ, by the display of compassion, and love for God and His people, this will draw other souls to Him. People wanted to be a part of this love show that was being displayed, which made them give their lives to God and join in. They desired the connection of who we are connected to, and what they saw displayed in our church.

We love as Christ loves, and in Christ Jesus, there are no strangers. God has already provided the resources and will continue to do so. We must have a desire for His people to dominate and have dominion in Christ Jesus; as we live, breathe, move, and have our total being.

July 1, 2017

Dream

My husband had a dream he was in his office at home with my sister Juanita and her son Damien. They were all talking then Damien pulled out a gun on him. Next, they went into the family room and he pointed the gun at me. My sister was just sitting by saying nothing. The gun was never released. No bullets came out. End of dream.

Interpretation

The dream started out in the office where my husband studies and hears from God. The enemy will try and use people to do harmful things to you. He uses people like Damien that have temporary fallen back from the Word. However, if you are continuing in God's Word and obeying him, He will shut down what the enemy tries to do through people.

My sister's silence was because she didn't know what to say or do to stop the enemy. She's been off track in being aware of the enemy's attack. We were never afraid of what was going on.

The enemy was and is afraid of us. As you noticed, the gun didn't release. No bullets fired. The weapons will be formed but they shall not prosper.

July 2, 2017

Dream

I was in a stretch limo. My daughter Tange and my grandson Josiah were in the seats behind me. The driver

I didn't recognize who he was. We were up high on the highway, or what looked like a bridge, and when he turned the corner it was really fast and the car went over the cliff, landing on the sand of a large beach. I noticed a European American man rescuing someone out of the water. Then he came over and rescued us from the car. End of dream.

Interpretation

Since God has conquered the enemy, we've received supernatural blessings that are coming our way. Expect nothing less. The enemy tried to stop us, but didn't succeed. God has blessed us indeed. Our territories are large because God has set us in this large place. Take notice it was a large beach surrounded by lots of water that is we couldn't see an ending. He reminded me of what He spoke in my book *T.S.I.T.S. Thing Seen In The Spirit,* on page 36-37 dated May 22nd which is my birthday. This explains all that's coming to us.

August 24, 2017

Dream

When I closed my eyes while praying in the spirit I saw this:

Big city at night with beautiful different color lights
An Angel playing a harp

Interpretation

Even in our darkest nights God allows our light to shine bright, it's beautiful for all the world to see. We are the show for the world to know, they will know where He has chosen for us to go. Continue to go yea therefore with compassion, calling, and compelling people to receive our Almighty God, the one who's blessing man and woman. He has given us all His promises, by grace, through faith.

There's a sweet sound played on a musical instrument that has strings stretched across a large open frame and its played with our fingers. God uses this particular instrument for example, because of its large frame, to show you how far you can stretch across this world when being obedient to His will. He uses the Angel the one who obeys our voice, and brings all things our way.

When we pray we always need to be ready to receive what God has to say.

> Know that God causes everything to work together for the good of those who love Him, and are called according to his purpose for them.
> **Romans 8:28 NLT**

November 9, 2017

Dream

In this dream I was living in a place where people were putting their things in back of my house, which cause it to look messy. I was led to look back there right after they had placed the stuff there. I knew who the people were, and I confronted them, and they were surprised that I knew it was them. I asked them to move the mess. As I entered the next part of this dream, someone said that this place where I was living, there were people that was kidnapping children. I immediately began to protect my family, and move away from this place. End of dream.

Interpretation

I must never allow people to dump their garbage on me. My eyes must be open to who and what's all around me. Garbage dumped behind me, says people are being messy behind my back, they are trying to hide what they are doing and saying about me. Kidnapping children, was about people trying to take the very things and people that I love. I was told, and I immediately took action because of the warning.

Everything was revealed, because I recognized the trash even though it was behind my house. I knew to look back there after they put it there. God exposes and reveals things to His people who are following His instructions. He gives us His wisdom, knowledge, and understanding of what to do, and we follow through. We are led by His Spirit. If I had not gone back there at the time He said go, I wouldn't have seen what was going on.

It's important to move at God command, and stand. Have strength to recognize and face the enemy, and his schemes, as he tries to put road blocks in your path to distract you from doing what God wants you to do. Never be distracted, disturbed, and disappointed, with what the enemy tries to destroy and send a decoy to stop you from reaching your destination. We must confront the enemy, tell him where to go, which is back to the pit of hell where he belongs.

Stand strong. Never give in, we have the winning hand. God has given us His plans. Plans to prosper us, and have the expected end. We win!

Dream

This was a short but sweet dream once I knew what the interpretation was. In this dream my husband and I was placed in this small room that was uncovered or didn't have doors. We had to pass by two other rooms that were opened and small. We immediately recognized this place was too small. Before we could say anything, someone came and said, "Oh no, this is too small for you."

She took us to another place that was very large. She said, "This is the place you should be in."

Pastor Timothy Moore walked in, and told us this was a nice place for us. He then began to speak with my husband about money. My husband received his wisdom and dream over.

Interpretation

God has placed us in a large place, and we can't receive small anymore. We recognize it and other people have also. They will cater to us and help us to continue to live in this large place. Pastor Moore was happy for us, and supported us as he gave us wisdom on money. We received.

February 9, 2018

Dream

In this dream I was out in a public place with my husband and others. We were taking turns praying. I was the last one to pray. I began to pray, and as I was praying, tears ran down my face, and I began to cry as I continued praying. There were people looking and staring, and people that were in agreement with the prayers. I felt such a pouring out and love for the people, and assurance that my prayers were answered and people received, as they had been released. Thank God for His people that know prayer is still needed. Thank you, Lord, for the release and using me!

Interpretation

God has charged me to pray prayers of release. God showed me that prayer is needed everywhere and we are not afraid to pray everywhere. We have been chosen to do the prayer work. Just because people were staring and looking, don't mean that they were not receiving, and that they didn't receive their release. The atmosphere was set for the release to come in, which allowed the people to win. The spirit of the Lord was moving as the release has begun. I decreed things and released the blood of Jesus to work on their behalf. People were set free.

All others prayed and my job was easy. I'm to step in and finish what was started. Like putting the icing on the cake. I'm confident and bold as a lion. I speak boldly, I'm boisterous as the wind, as I rely on Holy Spirit to step in. He speaks and pray through, and for me. I have a heart of love to help people receive. I thank God for other prayer warriors, that help bring people into the righteous place in the Kingdom of God. What an awesome dream.

March 5, 2018

Dream

I dreamed my husband showed me five one hundred dollars bills that we had. I found three more one hundred dollars bills that he didn't show me, the first time: then I came back again and showed him that I found five more one hundred-dollar bills he didn't show me again. I told him what was that about? Why I'm I finding more money than he's telling me we have? My first thought was, is he hiding money from me? Or, is he not seeing the money I'm seeing? Is he miscounting, or mishandling the money? Is this an honest mistake? Did he really not see this extra eight hundred dollars?

This is thirteen hundred dollars total, being mistaken for five hundred.

Interpretation

Money can't be hidden from me any longer. There's no amount of money that can be hidden because of the two different amounts. Each time the money increased, from three hundred then five hundred, by twos. God said, "This is how money will come to you." He's given me double for my trouble, because of what I've been through, and come through.

He continued on, saying: "I've worked it all out for you." I stopped writing and begin to give Him Praise! I bless His Holy name! The name above every name! The name that's always the same! The name that never will change! "Lord, I worship you!"

He continued to say that I will receive money like never before. "Money has found me, and it's revealed to me."

He said that I have been doing, and must continue to do my part, which is recognizing, and receiving money that has been revealed to me. God said my husband won't see the money that He's revealed to me to receive, and that the purpose of me showing him the money I found was because He wants him to see it's what He's placed in our hands through me.

God said to tell my husband to stop saying that I'm not working and that he's the only one going to work while I sit at home doing nothing. God said to continue in my prayer, praise and worship, as He continues to reveal His prophecies. He shall do nothing, except He will continue to reveal the secrets to His servants, the prophets: believe them and know that what they speak, has, and shall, continue to come from Me: and we will always receive His prosperity!"

God also showed me that even though I thought those things about my husband, like, him showing me one amount of money, and I found other amounts, I never accused him. I took control over my fleshly thoughts, and allowed them to be in subjection to my spiritual mind, which is in Christ Jesus.

When I live in the spirit I receive the things of the spirit. God desires for us to be rich and wealthy. It's already in our houses. It's no longer laid up for us, but it's been revealed and released to us so that we can recognize and receive it.

Never let the enemy take what He's already given us, by grace through faith, He's made the way, even when we couldn't see our way. Never worry about money ever again, because money will keep coming in. Never allow the enemy to keep us in sin, because He's designed us to win.

> "Let this mind be in you, which was also in Christ Jesus:"
> **Philippians 2:5 KJV**

> "For those who are living according to the flesh set their minds on the things of the flesh [which gratify the body], but those who are living according to the Spirit, [set their minds on] the things of the Spirit [His will and purpose]."
> **Romans 8:5 AMP**

> "And they rose early in the morning, and went forth into the wilderness of Tekoa: and as they went forth, Jehoshaphat stood and said, Hear me, O Judah, and ye inhabitants of Jerusalem; Believe in the Lord your God, so

shall ye be established; believe his prophets, so shall ye prosper."

2 Chronicles 20:20KJV

March 6, 2018

Dream

I was holding hands and kneeling down getting ready to pray with my family and my husband family, and right before prayer Pastor CC Hatter's phone rang it was Pastor McGhee from Chicago. He took the call instead of continuing on to pray with us. I thought to myself, is that call more important than praying with his family? I said to myself: "He could have waited, after all it was just a call that he could have answered after prayer." We ended up not praying at all after that. The next part of the dream, I was singing out loud, the words, good gifts and giving. I was very happy as I was singing this, in fact others were looking on, and listening.

Interpretation

When I woke up, I was so happy and joyous, and then a few minutes later, I began to pray on the Prayer Line. My prayer was all about giving, and how we should be releasing the seeds, and that everything rebounds back to us from our giving. Healing, and health. Our giving connects us to the guaranteed quality of life we live, which is in peace, protection, promises, promotions, provisions, prosperity and power from Gods Holy Spirit, that's He's promised and given to us.

God revealed in this dream that we can't allow nothing and no one to stop us and get us off track, even our loved ones. My father in law allowed the distraction and maybe even believed the phone call was more important than his family coming together in prayer. The fact that both families came together to pray was a blessing in itself. We never finished what we started, which was prayer, because we allowed him to get us off track. This must never happen. Especially something as vital as coming together in agreement in prayer.

God showed me, in the next part of this dream; that even though this happened, I was on track with my good gifts and giving. This dream was the next night, after He spoke to me about money. God said, "we can get off track if we don't stay focus and in faith, trusting and believing in Him to bring all things to past." Continue to give good gifts as unto the lord. Be happy and joyous in giving, not sad and sorry that we are commanded to give, because it will come back to us in every way more than what we gave out.

> "Give, and it will be given to you. They will pour into your lap a good measure--pressed down, shaken together, and running over [with no space left for more]. For with the standard of measurement you use [when you do good to others], it will be measured to you in return.
>
> **Luke 6:38 AMP**

March 14, 2018

Dream

In this dream I was driving with my son Tristian in the car with me. We was stopping at various places in the ministry, and some other places. Like New Light Church, and Pastor Cowend Church. All the places we went, people were welcoming us; happy to see us and asking to meet my son, Tristian. I introduced him to lots of people. Young people were excited to meet him. He was talking to them and they were asking him about when they were going to meet and get together this young people ministry group that would help the community and church as a whole.

He told everyone he would be back with details on what he's planning to do, and a list of who would assist him. One older gentlemen in particular was saying that he could help him and they could connect with United Airlines and bring the group together and take over the southern parts of the country.

As we continued on to the different stops, there were times when Tristian ended up in the driver's seat, and I noticed it right away and immediately said to him, "You are not supposed to be driving, I am." I told him he didn't know the area well enough to be driving, and we changed seats.

There was one time when Tristian was already driving and I didn't notice it right away. He was speeding down this dead-end street, which was known to be in a bad neighborhood. At the end of this street was a lot of water that looked liked a flood. I took over the driving from that point on.

We went down this one street and an elderly woman tried to force her way into the car, while someone at the front door was calling her to come back. I got her out the way, and she felled down into the street almost being ran over by oncoming car. We continued on to our other stops. When we stopped at New Light Church, I was on this high platform-like thing and was really high up. All were happy to see us, except Mrs. Bobbie, who was more concerned about the platform thing I was on. She was saying I wasn't supposed to be in there with her on this platform. I told her Dr. Ireashea said that I looked great on it and had no problem with me being on it.

I saw these elder and younger women dressed up like the traditional church people usually dressed. They were very receptive of me on this platform, and they said, "We got your back, and that, Mrs. Bobbie was out of order with what she was saying to me. When we left out of there, we saw Mrs. Bobbie again standing on the corner of New Light Church looking confused. I told her how she treated me in there wasn't nice. She agreed and said whatever I needed she would help me.

The next part of the dream I was backing out from a parking spot and this man deliberately hit me from the back. I was trying to get Tristan's attention, but he had earplugs in and he couldn't hear me. Afterwards, I told him he need to pay attention and not shut off from what's going on. I could have been hurt by this person and he wouldn't have seen it. End of dream.

Interpretation

Tristian and I are going places together, where people are always happy and excited to see us. Tristian isn't quite ready for the great task ahead of him yet. He has some training and growing up to do. He's called to lead massive young people, and help build up the kingdom of God. The team God has prepared is excited and ready to assist him. God has elevated me to this high platform and position in His Kingdom: and the ones who matter will except me, and the ones I thought would be happy for me, won't be at first, however they will soon realize, it's all God, and they will do what God has told them concerning me.

March 26, 2018

Dream

In the dream I was sleeping in the guest room and I heard the door open. Assuming it was Maranda, my granddaughter, I called her name. When I didn't hear anything, so I closed the door back. The door opened back up so I took Josiah, my grandson and went out the room to look for her.

When I went in my room, she was still in bed and woke up when I sat down. She told me there was a boy in my spot before I sat down and he got close to her face.

She turned around and went back to sleep and I saw a little boy about 5 or 6 floating above her.

When I asked who he was he said he didn't know and that he only knew me. I turned around and there were pictures of kids posted on my headboard. One picture looked like me as a kid with a few others and a baby boy. The boy told me he had to get to me through Maranda because I couldn't see him. I woke up inside the dream and was back in the guest room. My subconscious was aware that I was still dreaming, and I began shaking my dream self and eventually was able to wake myself up in real life.

Interpretation

Maranda will reach or draw children in her age group to the Kingdom of God. Tange has to continue obeying God and getting up and doing her part, to keep Maranda focused and bringing children into the kingdom of God. The children will recognize who Tange is and want to be close to her, but they will be drawn in by Maranda. The lifting up of the boy was salvation; and children all around the head board of the bed, represents the compassion and love of Tange and Maranda that will keeps drawing lots of children in. Praise God!!! Hallelujah!!!

April 27, 2018

Dream

I was communicating with a female African American doctor, explaining the different things about buying houses and how to get approved for them. The doctor asked me about being a realtor.

The next part of this dream I was in my home, organizing things in my computer as if I was already a realtor, but I didn't have license yet. I was talking about being a realtor. While I was talking, I saw this women laying hands on my daughter, Tange. I went and stood behind her and whispered in her ear that she wasn't to allow anyone to suddenly lay hands on her. I told her she had enough in her and she knew her purpose.

The next part of this dream I was in a church service where a female was teaching and this was our church because there were women on both sides of me and one of them said, "First Lady why are you not sitting on the second row?" There were women all around the church praying with their shoes off and white cloths under their feet. Some women were standing and praying, and others were kneeling down praying. They all had white cloths under them. One of the women that was sitting next to me tried to add her teachings and interrupt the lady that was teaching. I said to her, "I'm sure you have a good lesson, but this isn't your turn." She listened and didn't interrupt.

Interpretation

I'm to help all women, and not just the poor ones. I'm to help women of higher standards and good jobs also. I will lead them to the house of the lord, where there are other prayer warriors all around, praying for them. Some women will be watchful and praying, and others will be kneeling down and listening to God while praying.

All women will be interceding in prayer. I will keep order in God's house and people will listen. I've been given GCW ministry to help women of all calibers, or walks of life. I've been charged to continue what He's allowed me to start. Women will come from near and far, to be a part of GCW ministry. Women will be willing to help me, by listening to what God has spoken to them, and what He's called me to do: which is build up women and teach them how to live life in the spirit and in the natural.

The realtor job was about helping women find their natural home, or place of purpose, and their spiritual home or place of purpose. Meaning building up their character, physically and spiritually.

June 2, 2018

Dream

In this dream I was standing next to my son Tristian. I looked down and saw a cat and a snake at my feet. I wasn't afraid of it and I shook it off and told my son that the snake was there. The cat was trying to get a grip on the snake but couldn't.

Tristian wasn't concerned about getting rid of the snake he just was picking up the cat. The snake got bigger and I saw it hiding under the concrete. Tristian said he couldn't see the snake nor was he concerned about it, he kept trying to play with the cat and hold on to it.

I removed myself from him and got out the way of the snake. He was still holding the cat and I woke up.

Interpretation

I recognized the enemy that was at my feet and I immediately got rid of him. My son however didn't seem to care about the enemy because he was busy holding on to the female that can't help him, because she's busy doing what he's doing, and that's why she couldn't get a grip or hold on the enemy.

The snake got bigger meaning, the enemy got stronger because he was distracted and didn't want to defeat the enemy even though I was trying to help him, telling him about the enemy. I can't defeat the enemy for him and he has to want to defeat him.

I saw he didn't want to change and separated myself from him. He wanted to hold on to what he thought was good, the female. I had to let go and I did. We can only help those who want the help regardless of who they are. We love our children however they have to love God and obey Him: this is the only way they will recognize and defeat the enemy. This is choice driven.

Dream

I was in this hotel conference room where I saw this woman and she told me that she owned the hotel. Holy Ghost led me to minister to this women. She didn't look sick; however, she had a disease. I casted the disease out and told her she was healed, and not to let the disease return. I encountered more women that were looking on as I casted out the disease. I told them I was the real deal and that I was a demon buster. My daughter Tange said, "Yes she is," and smiled and walked off.

At this time, I hadn't told anyone who I was, even my name. These women stared following me around as I began walking around the room. I encountered this one woman that was unsure and doubted who I was. I began to lay hands on her and pray in the Holy Ghost first. I then started casting out demons from her that had held her down for years. Still, these other women kept following me and looking on, listening and hearing what was taking place.

As time went on, my daughter Tange decided to leave without letting me know she was gone. When I finished I didn't have my phone and needed a ride. I asked one of the women that had been following me around to drop me off where Tange was. I told her I would give her gas money she said ok. She dropped me off at another hotel that didn't look like the correct place to me, that I wanted to go to. The woman said this is the place.

So, after I got there I saw men with knives at people throats. Still these same women somehow were following and looking listening and hearing. One man came up to me with a knife and I began to pray in the Holy Ghost and cast out evil spirits from him. The other men that was with him was afraid and dropped their knives. They all stared at me as I prayed for everyone, and invited them to KMC.

The woman that dropped me off there asked for her gas money, and I gave her double of what she asked for. She said you not only the real deal but you got lots of money. I knew I had their attention now, and that's when I told them that I was the First Lady of KMC. I ministered to them and they listened and received Christ right at that moment. Wow! End of dream. Awesome ending!!!

Interpretation

I will begin to be in the presence of women that will follow me to see what's to me at first. God will allow His miracles of healing, deliverance, and money to come forth immediately, for all people to see, male and female. I'm not afraid of no devils. I've been taken to higher levels in Christ Jesus.

Some people will be unsure at first but the power and anointing that's on me, will cause them to follow me. Signs and wonder shall follow also. In Jesus name I shall cast out demons and they will flee. People will be set free. People will be saved in Jesus Christ name. Their lives will never be the same. They will believe because of what they see.

I will continue to walk in who God called me to be. The sick will be healed and money will continue to be received. All because of the Kingdom work that will be done by me. Miracles, signs, and wonders will keep following me, as Apostle has already prophesied to me. It's already happening now. I will just keep believing Gods prophet so will I continue to prosper. I shall teach others how to follow, as some don't know how, right now.

The ones that I think knows how to follow will need more teaching. They must learn to not go on their own without me, and hear God continually. I must stay focused, in faith, and continue to watch finances come my way. People will come to the kingdom of God by the masses.

November 10, 2018

Dream

I had this dream about my uncle Cliff, which has gone on to be with the lord. In this dream he took an organ that I had at my home to our church. I told him to be careful and take care of my organ. Don't damage it.

Interpretation

I know now that my praise is in my house and God has allowed someone precious to me to assist me in taking it to the church. Make sure your praise can't be damaged or destroyed. Take care in praise. When your praise is to God, you will receive and all who will connect in praise to Him will also receive.

May 2019

Tange Dream

My daughter Tange dreamed that she was at a funeral, sitting on front row, and three ladies which she considered to be her close friends came to her and whispered something in her ear. Then they went away. End of dream.

Interpretation

This dream was to let Tange know she been elevated but separated. Her sitting on the front row was elevation and the three friends she has to separate from. They came to her and whispered in her ear. They left afterwards. They are not a part of where God has taken her and she must listen to Holy Spirit, that whisper, that quite still voice instructing her to separate from people that she considered to be her close friends however they aren't ready to move forward in the direction that God has elevated her to, and allows her to travel down His straight and narrow path.

This is the place that all will not go. This place that's promised. She must allow Holy Spirit to lead, show, and she must follow.

May 20, 2019

Dream

In this dream there were people from my past and others that I didn't know. We were on the balcony looking down on people paying close attention to what was going on in our surroundings. We were in a church service which involved people teaching and preaching. There was lots of people attending this event.

My Uncle Cliff was in this dream and I was told by someone that Apostle Hilliard was there, however I didn't see him. The person said he was in the back away from everyone. I came down from the balcony because it was time for people to pray and I was one of the prayer warriors.

We lined up in twos. Immediately when I came down I saw a large amount of water filling up on the floor and looking as though it would flood the floor. I told my uncle Cliff about the water and he said "he saw it but it wasn't gone do any damage." I was looking for my partner for prayer and she or he wasn't there. I chose another person and was ready for prayer. End of dream.

Interpretation

God has elevated me and allowed me to see things from a higher level and pay close attention to what's happening around me and what type of people that's in my surroundings. He has people that are from my past who will assist me in building up His Kingdom.

I don't have to worry about the things that seem to be flooding or coming up against me, He's my protector. I must have peace knowing He's giving me the discernment and I see what's gone happen before it happens. Holy Spirit is always with me, helping me to see.

I must focus on the task that He has for me, and continue to be who He wants me to be regardless of what I see. I must obey Him at all times and all cost. His work will be done and people that has been there before me and walking in His will, they are watching behind the scene. It's about always being obedient to God at all times regardless of who's watching. Don't stop obeying God because people aren't. There's always others ready and willing to obey, so that the task at hand will be done anyway.

Dream

My husband dreamed about his childhood friend and his cousin that has died. In this dream they were talking to him. They were asking him why he didn't tell them certain things that he had done. Dream over.

Interpretation

Old things in his life has passed away and behold all things are new. Things that has been a waste in his life and he thought that they were God's will, He's allowed those things to be washed away. Things and people that we love we have to be willing to let go of, then we can receive from heaven above. Some things we can't tell, even if they are your best friends. Wait patiently on God to bring it all to pass. In our waiting follow Holy Ghost lead and obey God by walking in His paths.

Dream

Sharika Hooper was in my home, and every room I was in, she was there also. There was a time where I saw her come in one room and I said no, wait, this is not the room to come into. You're not supposed to be in here. She was asking what could she do for me and I was directing her about the kingdom. Letting her know it's God first and while it's okay to honor men and women of God,

He must be the one who instructs us on how to honor them.

She was protective of me and made sure no one came into my space except she checked them out and said they were good. I said to her you have to be a great follower before you can be a great leader. Her two younger sons were in the house with her. They asked can they go into the family room and watch television with their dad. She said Asia was on the way.

Interpretation

She's supposed to be a part of KMC helping build up the kingdom right now. Her family follows when she's certain of what to do. Her sons being there watching her however they wanted to be with the father too. Both Sharika and James must be in agreement on the move and the children will be feel comfortable working in the kingdom doing what they like to do.

Dream

I had a dream husband and I was with our attorney signing our check for the lawsuit. It was over $200,000. They had to swab or mouths. We agreed to pay off both vehicles and the chase credit card. Husband said he would sow about $1500 each SMC2U Conferences, and said it would feel good sowing consistently. I was dreaming while I was dreaming, and I heard him say, "Money cometh to me now. Money just keeps on coming to me now." I woke up from the dream.

Interpretation

In this particular dream God gave me the interpretation before I wrote down the dream. I was dreaming in my dream.

My dreams have come to pass and they last. I've received my dreams and God allows me to continue dreaming. He showed me that while I was in the natural sleeping, I went into the spirit realm and received what I have been desiring and speaking in the natural realm, and He has allowed it to manifest to me now, and I can see it. After I woke up, I heard Apostle Leroy Thompson saying, "money that has been held up is released to us now." I heard him also say, "go back to where you've been told no and you'll receive your yes." I thanked God and I received!

I heard these scriptures as I was writing down the interpretation.

> In the year that King Uzziah died, I saw [in a vision] the Lord sitting on a throne, high and exalted, with the train of His royal robe filling the [most holy part of the] temple.
>
> **Isaiah 6:1 AMP**

> So they got up early in the morning and went out into the Wilderness of Tekoa; and as they went out, Jehoshaphat stood and said, "Hear me, O Judah, and you inhabitants of Jerusalem! Believe and trust in the LORD your God and you will be established (secure). Believe and trust in His prophets and succeed.

2 Chronicles 20:20 AMP

I also heard Apostle Leroy Thompson say, things will happen quickly for us. Immediately, straightway, and suddenly. Here's the scripture he gave us.

> Yes indeed, it won't be long now." GOD 's Decree. "Things are going to happen so fast your head will swim, one thing fast on the heels of the other. You won't be able to keep up. Everything will be happening at once—and everywhere you look, blessings! Blessings like wine pouring off the mountains and hills. I'll make everything right again for my people Israel:
>
> They'll rebuild their ruined cities. They'll plant vineyards and drink good wine. They'll work their gardens and eat fresh vegetables. And I'll plant them, plant them on their own land. They'll never again be uprooted from the land I've given them." GOD, your God, says so.
>
> **Amos 9:13-15 MSG**

> "When the chief baker saw that the interpretation [of the dream] was good, he said to Joseph, "I also dreamed, and [in my dream] there were three cake baskets on my head;"
>
> **Genesis 40:16 AMP**

Increase!

September 8, 2019

Dream

I was at a service at Lebanon Church in Chicago, Pastor Kenneth Jackson. Before the service ended the lord told me to tell Evangelist Sharon Jackson that I have a word for the people, and there's some things that needed to be revealed and casted out. Immediately she said yes. She started preparing for me to minister.

While she was preparing I was just sitting quietly and I saw a long clear like pipe with a black snake coming out of it. It bit this man and then it bit me, however I wasn't affected or afraid of it. This snake was hiding out behind a furnace in the basement of their church.

People were saying to me that they heard I was bitten by this snake, and I told them yes, but I was good. It didn't hurt me.

There was this tall, light skinned lady that I saw in the dream and this short dark skinned man asking me what was my message gone be about. I told them I would teach on the Holy Spirit and Holy Spirit would lead me through. Evangelist Jackson told me that she was waiting on some more people to show up, and she was asking each person to invite at least five quests.

Evangelist Jackson said these words to me, "I don't know why you been sitting in the background so long and not using your gift, I saw who you were years ago, now people about to know who you are, the enemy knows you, that's why he tried to stop you back then by distracting you, it was never about what your husband was going through."

I was alone praying in the Holy Ghost, and as I was praying I felt such an anointing on me, and an urgency to get God word out and do His work. Powerful. After I stopped praying, I saw Angela Jackson, my husband's cousin. I told her she definitely needed to be in this service and that there would be an awesome move of God taking place. She was excited and said yes, she would be there. People began to fill up the Church. My husband was there however he didn't know that I was gone minister. This had been a long day at the church but everyone that was already there stayed. They was hungry for the word, and ready to hear and receive what God was gone do through me. They knew I was bitten by this snake and not affected. End of dream.

Interpretation

The lord is about to make me an open show for the world to know. He's using people that are willing to help the Kingdom grow. The demons have been disguised long enough. It's time for them to be revealed. God is about to use the ones that's real and ready to walk in His will. He is going to use the ones that are not afraid or those that won't allow themselves to be affected by his poison.

The enemy has been hidden to long. He's been hidden right under people, and they weren't aware of just how close he was. They thought they had power but they were only using part of what God had given them.

They had been sitting on their gifts and trying to help with other people's gifts. They hadn't been displaying and recognizing their strengths, authority, and power.

God has been waiting on them a long time. He's been in their presence but they've been leaving Him without their answers and deliverance. They have been covering up, what they couldn't and didn't know what to cast out, cancel, curse, and correct.

Even though the enemy tries he won't succeed. He can't harm me. I recognize who's in need of and finally who's gone succeed. Those that want to come out will come forth. It's been tough and rough. They're excited because they have accepted that they are in need of change. They will receive in Jesus name. They will never be the same.

People who are helping me to advance the kingdom will be excited and know that I'm sent by God, and they will appreciate me. People will be healed, delivered, and set free, by the hands of God almighty! He's using me. He's ready to use others to, and this is why they're being set free. I praise God for the increase.

November 17, 2019

Dream

I had this dream about being at this place that had a back entrance with lots of snow. There weren't any stairs, but I stepped down into the snow and my feet landed straight in at the path that I needed to walk. Then people followed behind me when they saw the path was clear. Then I moved to a part of the dream where there was like a beach, sand, and lots of water with no ending.

The last part of dream was Oprah Winfrey walking to her car with her assistant. I asked her if I could be first in line outside of this big building with different entrances. Looked like a church. She turned around and begin to lay hands on people and they were falling. People thought she was crazy and I said she was filled with Holy Spirit and it's real. Dream over.

Interpretation

God is allowing me to walk in His paths. Things that's not normal to the world they will begin to see and follow Him from my example and leadership. The supernatural is operating now in my life and the things in the past that wasn't working for me, I've worked hard at obtaining the finer things in life. This new life in Christ has allowed me to excel to higher levels and so can you. The world won't understand except they give Christ their life and begin to change now. Things happened quick.

November 24, 2019

Dream

I dreamed I was living in this mansion that had a care taker. I was having a special event but not sure what it was for. The actress Lisa Raye was in my master bathroom. I told her this was my personal space and she shouldn't have been in there. I mentioned this to the care taker for her to make sure no one is where they shouldn't be in my home. After that happened, the care taker informed me that Lisa Raye was telling people that this was her home. I told the care taker if she continues with this she would be asked to leave.

Next part of dream I was in a car race and I won. The prize was monetary. I remembered waking up right before 5am and saying thank you lord for my money.

Interpretation

God has quickly released the many mansion as He said He would. We have to be ready to receive and live according to His will for our lives. We must not allow people with titles and influence to invade our private space just because of who they are. We must take authority right away, and bring correction. Don't allow anyone to claim our wealth regardless of who that are.

What God has given us is for us, and we are the only ones that can give it away, no one can take it or claim it for themselves.

I had to get in the race in order to win it. How I entered into the race was important. I entered in it with confidence, faith, and expectation that I would win, and I did. I won the money that was waiting on me. Miracle money has manifested to me now. I didn't know how, however I had faith to believe it was for me and coming to me. We have to do everything in our power to go and get what God has given us according to His power and will for us. I believed, and I received the increase that was for me. Thank God!

November 29, 2019

Dream

First thing happened I was at church listening to a female preaching. She finished up and sat next to me asking if she did good or did I enjoy the message. She said she wanted to get more people following and listening to her. I told her don't be concerned with the people listening and following her.

I told her to make sure she's doing her work as unto the lord and He makes room for her gift. I told her it's been 12 years for me teaching and staying focus on what God wants me to do for real. There were times I didn't understand how or what to do but now I'm in line with what God wants me to do, and told her He will do the same for you. Just obey Him in all you do. People will let you down but God will always be around.

The next part of the dream, Angela Jackson came to this same service but showed up late. I told her service was almost over and she needed to get to church on time. I was standing down at the right side of the alter and she gave me a flower pot running over with water and she said this was her gift to me. I said put it in the back so water don't spill out on the floor in the church. The secretary of Lebanon, who is a light skinned lady, came with a gift also.

Other ladies from Lebanon begin to come and give me gifts also. I begin talking with evangelist Jackson and telling her I was sent by God to them. She responded she knew because she saw me in a vision, we talked about what God wanted to do through us and training was necessary for them, just like I had to be trained.

She said she was tired but wanted to make sure the church was in great hands, and she didn't want the pastor's legacy to be in vain. They worked too hard. We went to the dining area to eat. Pastor was eating and I asked him where was my plates? Someone went to make sure I got a plate. He said he thought I had eaten. I said next time make sure. End of dream.

December 12, 2019

Dream

I was driving on the highway and I came upon someone that said slow down there's something ahead but they weren't sure what it was. As I proceeded I came into a large body of water with lots of people in different areas of it. I immediately retained me an area in this large body of water.

I was comfortable and had no worries. I was happy and I said this is a really nice place to be. It was if the whole community was happy, peaceful, and the ones that were there belonged there. Even though it was so much water, no one went under we all stayed at the top of it. It's like something was supernaturally keeping us at the top. End of dream.

Interpretation

This large body of water represents the supernatural. I wasn't aware of the time when the blessings came, I just drove right into them. Because of patiently waiting, God has allowed His obedient children to rest and relax, be comfortable, happy, and at peace with His supernatural blessings. No one can take them away, and they won't cause us to go under. We will never be in a survival mode. As we relax we shall see the blessings as they unfold. I was told to slow down and that something was ahead of me. This was for me, and God didn't want me to miss out on what He had already set up for me. Sometimes we are moving in areas we don't know and God wants us to slow down so we can see where to go. Once we come upon the place to be, He will allow us to see and receive. He says, "Enjoy the blessings from Me, and you are right where I want you to be."

I received these blessings as I was just driving along. This happened when I was right where I belonged. I was alone with Him and no one else with me that would have panicked, or said "turn around because this would have slowed us down." Again, God made sure I didn't miss what He had released to me.

It's good to be in His presence all the time with no distractions. We must obey, never be led astray, and go our own way. Our way seems to be right sometimes, but it could lead us into wrong paths and destinations that wasn't set up for us from God. He assures and shows us doing things His way causes us to stay. Stay in His promises, provisions, promotions, and prosperity. All these things gives Him pleasure.

December 20, 2019

Dream

This was a short dream. I was lying down with arms by my side, husband lying to my left also. A white cat ran passed my left arm in between us, and I jumped and jerked hard and fast enough to where it woke me up. My husband made a joke and said you jerking like you in the supermarket. This was something our Apostle Leroy Thompson said years ago. I told him that I felt that jerk also.

Interpretation

White cats symbolize wealth and riches. Being that I jerked because I couldn't jump at the time while laying down. This cat ran pass which means the wealth gone come fast. Like the scripture says here.

> "Yes indeed, it won't be long now." GOD 's Decree. "Things are going to happen so fast your head will swim, one thing fast on the heels of the other. You won't be able to keep up. Everything will be happening at once— and everywhere you look, blessings! Blessings like wine pouring off the mountains and hills. I'll make everything right again for my people Israel: "They'll rebuild their ruined cities. They'll plant vineyards and drink good wine. They'll work their gardens and eat

> fresh vegetables. And I'll plant them, plant them on their own land. They'll never again be uprooted from the land I've given them." GOD, your God, says so."
>
> **Amos 9:13-15 MSG**

We were just lying there relaxed not caring or worried about anything, even though bills are due and late. We have settled in our hearts, believe, expect, and know that God has already released His promises by grace through faith. The way has already been made. Even when we couldn't see a way out. We continue to shout. Knowing that God has brought us out.

God will allow you to relax in the storms of life. Our sowing seeds have been a sacrifice. Our seeds are a memorial to God. He remembers every one of them, and they will always work for us. We've given with purpose and from the heart, as this scripture says:

> "Let each one give [thoughtfully and with purpose] just as he has decided in his heart, not grudgingly or under compulsion, for God loves a cheerful giver [and delights in the one whose heart is in his gift]."
>
> **2 Corinthians 9:7 AMP**

And God is able to make all grace [every favor and earthly blessing] come in abundance to you, so that you may always [under all circumstances, regardless of the need] have complete sufficiency in everything [being completely self-sufficient in Him], and have an abundance for every good work and act of charity."

2 Corinthians 9:8 AMP

February 13, 2020

Dream

I had a dream Apostle Hilliard was teaching he was stopped by a lady and then went to the back and gave the man some money, came back, and preceded to teach. After he finished teaching, Pastor AD began teaching.

He was interrupted by a phone call from the man's wife who received the money from Apostle Hilliard. He stopped and talked to her, and afterwards preceded to teach. God said the most important thing in the Kingdom is the reach and then the teach. Of course, things will be done descent and in order. Holy Ghost order. We must meet the needs of the people.

What good is teaching and preaching and no one is helped, or even know what's their next step. The next part of this dream, the lady that interrupted Apostle Hilliard was in the lady's room with me, alone with the man that received the money. She was saying to him, "I told you God would make away."

He said, "I believe this stuff now."

I told her, "That a man shouldn't be in the lady's room," and they left.

I went back into the sanctuary where pastor AD Hatter was teaching. It was really bright and beautiful in there. As I looked around, I said, "This feels nice and it looks good in here." It was filled with lots of people. All races, and all kinds of people. People were dressed up, some were casual, and some were dressed down. Others looked as though they needed help buying clothes. It was an awesome atmosphere. I said, "God is here." Dream over.

Interpretation

God wants us to come together for His cause and not ours. Recognize who's in our churches, who's in need, and provide help with the need. Show love and kindness, regardless of your race and that of other people. However, we must have money to help people that's in need. Don't be so busy teaching and preaching that you forget what your job in the Kingdom is all about.

Do the work of Jesus. As he went about preaching and teaching he took out time to help those in need. He feed the five thousand women and children. God wants us in place to help the human race. It's not about the color of their face. It's not about how much money they have. Rich or poor He's opened all doors. Money shall keep coming in, to help us all win. Win the souls. Do as we are told. Watch His blessings unfold.

His wisdom from Holy Ghost, we must always behold. We gotta hear from God on every move we make, and every step we take. As long as He allows every breath, we must walk in faith. We must have insight, and love Him with all our might. We see far beyond what the world sees. We are blessed indeed. Our coasts have been enlarged. Make sure our reach is far greater than our teach and preach. Look first, and then we can see what God sees. We must allow Holy Ghost to lead us in the field. Meet the need. Feed the flock.

You can't be blocked or stopped. God's will and work will, and is being done. Do the work we've been called and commanded. Work every hand He's given us. We have received a winner's hand. Walk in His plans. He will always allow us to stand. Discerning and knowing what's in the enemy's hand. Again, having insight and faith. The angels are employed to hear what God, and His people say. They bring all His promises to us every day.

The heavens are open. God has spoken. Receive our fullness, fruitfulness, fatness, and fountains with a continual flow. We will now begin to walk in health and wealth like never before. Obey, and stay in place.

Always be ready to be used by God at all times. Your lights will continue to shine all the time. Keep walking in His Divine. His Trinity.

Conclusion

I thank God for giving me these Dreams and Interpretations. This is another gift from Him that I gladly accepted and shall continue to obey. I speak His revealed revelations by way of His Holy Spirit. I have clearly explained what He wants people to receive from Him, and they must reflect on, remember, and retain.

I thank God and His Holy Ghost for helping me to know everything, that these dreams mean, as I bring His word on the scene. Even though the enemy tried to intervene, people will know what Gods word mean.

These Dreams and Interpretations are from different people and events; however, God wants us to know just what's meant — meaning His will is for us to be able to take what's being said and use it as a guide in our lives.

Each dream is an example or eye opener that brings about a change, a correction, or challenge in our lives. We have to take what God has given to us. Hear, listen, and do, what He's spoken to and for you. Know that all things work together for the good, to those who are the called according to His purpose.

> "And we know [with great confidence] that God [who is deeply concerned about us] causes all things to work together [as a plan] for good for those who love God, to those who are called according to His plan and purpose."
> **Romans 8:28 AMP**

Your dreams have a purpose and a lesson for the blessings. Build His Kingdom first. Don't be blinded by your thoughts or the enemy thoughts. Don't allow the barrenness, brokenness, and bad things you might experience, to cause you not to receive all Gods blessings that He's released to you by grace through faith. Pay close attention and don't miss out on the message that's tailored for you.

Listen up as well as listen in. These Dreams come for you to win. Take what seems bad and use for your good. If things seem like they are on pause or delay, just wait patiently and they will soon come your way. Your dilemma is only an indication that your desires and destiny will quickly and suddenly reach the finish line in time. God is never late.

Now, receive what He's spoken to and through me. Again, I thank Him for using me. Gods prophets, you must believe. You shall receive prosperity and succeed. Know that my prayer and decree, is that we are blessed indeed. Repeat this with me. You will soon see. Remember don't cease to sow seeds. Plant your seeds in good soil today. Expect your harvest to come every day. Blessings always!

> "So they got up early in the morning and went out into the Wilderness of Tekoa; and as they went out, Jehoshaphat stood and said, "Hear me, O Judah, and you inhabitants of Jerusalem! Believe and trust in the LORD your God and you will be established (secure). Believe and trust in His prophets and succeed.""
>
> **2 Chronicles 20:20 AMP**

About the Author

Introducing Lady Mary Hatter

Hello everyone this is Lady Mary Hatter, and this is the day that the Lord has made, I will rejoice and be glad in it! Welcome and thank you for reading. I'd love to hear from you. Go to my website and send me an email.

I can say that God keeps blessings me and He has made my name great. So, it's never a coincidence with God — He knows and sees all. Therefore, my seeing, hearing, and understanding is as He wants it to be, and I decree the same for you!

Look at what these scriptures say...

These are the scriptures He gave me:

> Surely the Lord God will do nothing, but he revealeth his secret unto his servants the prophets.
>
> **Amos 3:7 KJV**

> Thus speaketh the Lord God of Israel, saying, Write thee all the words that I have spoken unto thee in a book.
>
> **Jeremiah 30:2 KJV**

> The prophet which prophesieth of peace, when the word of the prophet shall come to pass, then shall the prophet be known, that the Lord hath truly sent him.
>
> **Jeremiah 28:9 KJV**

> "It is written in the prophets, And they shall be all taught of God. Every man therefore that hath heard, and hath learned of the Father, cometh unto me."
>
> **John 6:45 KJV**

As You Journey

> And I will make of thee a great nation, and I will bless thee, and make thy name great; and thou shalt be a blessing:
>
> **Genesis 12:2 KJV**

Obeying Gods Law

> And He took the children [one by one] in His arms and blessed them [with kind, encouraging words], placing His hands on them.
>
> **Mark 10:16 AMP**

Who I'm I? Well here's my BIO:

Beautiful
Intelligent
Obedient

First and foremost, I'm a Woman of God who loves God and His people. I'm a loving wife, mother of two, Tangeneva and Tristian. I'm a grandmother of two, Maranda and Josiah. Better known as MaDiva to my grandchildren. I walk in several callings of God. Here they are: I'm a Prayer Warrior, Teacher, Preacher, Prophet, Praiser, and Worshipper, I'm the First Lady of KMC, Kingdom Minded Church, where I assist my husband Pastor AD Hatter, in building up God's Kingdom.

At KMC we purpose to do these three things:
- Train The Saints
- Teach The Scriptures
- Trust The Savior

Pastor and I serve under the leadership of Apostle Leroy Thompson Sr. We are connected to LTMA family: Leroy Thompson Ministerial Association. I'm the founder of GCW Ministry, God's CHASED Women, a women's fellowship that meets once a month or when time permits. I teach women how to love and support each another. We learn how to live effective, efficient, and excellent lives, so that we will experience all that God has already promised us, by grace through faith. I have several accomplishments; which includes, business owner, mentor, Author Coach, and I'm an Award-Winning Author. I received this Literary Award from Apostle IV and Pastor Bridget Hilliard, founders of the AIM Association. This award was for my first book, TSITS, *Things Seen In The Spirit*.

Lastly, I was born in a small town in Arkansas, by the name of Osceola. Most of my childhood and adult life I resided in Chicago, Illinois. In December of 2005, my husband, my daughter, and I relocated to Houston, Texas, and now, together with the grandchildren we live in Spring, Texas, which is considered the north suburban area, outside of Houston, Texas.

Allow me to further introduce myself by saying...

I'm created by God, fearfully and wonderfully made. I continue to be all that He wants me to be. I shall continue to possess all that God has already promised by grace through faith. I have set myself in agreement with God, Jesus, Holy Spirit, His people, and His word, and I purpose to obey everything from Him, that I've heard. I serve and I seek God's Kingdom first and His righteousness.

I receive everything He has done, is doing, and continues to do, as He adds to me. I allow God's Holy Spirit to work in me, through me, and for me. I command, cancel, and curse from the root everything the enemy has done or tries to do. I command the angels to bring all God's promises to me.

I'm a rejoicing and exceedingly glad servant. I'm happy in doing what God has called, commissioned, and commanded me to do. I thank God He's allowed me to release two new books: *Dreams What Are They and What Do They Mean?* and *ICU: Induced Comma Unconscious—Will You Wake Up?* I'm so excited about these two books!!! Of course, I feel that way about the others books as well.

I appreciate and thank you for your help in getting God's word out by purchasing your copies of my books. I trust that you love God unconditionally, as I do.

As I pray in the Holy Ghost daily, and afterwards I take time to listen to what He has to say. While listening to God I heard TSITS. I asked Him what does that mean? Later, He told me what the initials were. Those who know me know that when I teach, I use acronyms and initials a lot. This is how God speaks to me at times.

He told me I was His author, and He would give me what to say by way of His Holy Spirit. I just obey Him. He gave me these scriptures as a confirming word from Him. That's what God does He always gives a confirming word.

**If you enjoyed this book,
please check out Lady Mary's other books:**

The Secrets Are Out:
Nothing Happens Until the Secrets Are Revealed!

This powerful and awesome book will allow you to live and love life. Even though you might face troubled situations in life, God has allowed you to know what His Word says about it. You can come through everything that comes against you, when you obey what He says to do. God's secrets revealed are for you to rest, reign, rule, remain, and receive.

Book of Revelations: Divine Disclosures of Best Kept Secrets!:

This is another awesome book of revealed secrets from God, which He has blessed me to write, and I know it will bless the body of Christ. Believers must believe these two key truths: 1) God is NOT a man. 2) God DOES NOT lie.

T.S.I.T.S.: Things Seen in the Spirit

God is so awesome! He has allowed me to hear from Him like never before. As I pray daily and communicate with God and begin to listen to Him; He shares secrets with me to be revealed to the world. First God speaks what He wants to happen, how He wants it done and who He wants to do His work.

Confessions Journal: God's Word Spoken in Faith,
Believing that He Will Bring it to Pass,
According to His Will for Our Lives:

Lady Mary Hatter's writing will inspire you, as she shares secrets from God through confessions spoken to her by His

Spirit... Confessions from this book will help you to receive everything you want in the Kingdom and everything you want in every area of your life, your family and friend's lives.

God's Decrees Spoken By Me, I Receive!
Thank You Lord, for the Increase!

This awesome book of Decrees will teach you what to speak and how to receive. This book allows you to speak His promotions, promises, provisions, peace and prosperity. This book also speaks revelations, restoration, redemption, and helps reassign and realign things in your life.

In this book you will learn how to live and love life by speaking out your mouths what God says, and do what He says do, so that all His blessings shall keep coming to you. We decree manifestations, because we are a blessed generation and generations to come. It is God's will being done. Decrees are for our victory, and for all the world to see. We have His-story! We are made in His image. So is Jesus, so are we: because of His Decrees, we can and will live in prosperity! Receive all these Decrees!

Water Breaking Faith:
The Aftermath of Hurricane Harvey's Path

Praise God! I'm so overwhelmed with joy; even though the enemy sent a decoy. God's people are being led and fed by His Spirit, therefore the devil can't destroy.

As we continue to walk in willingness and obedience, we continue to eat the good of the land. We can never be destroyed by the pestilence and predators in these perilous times of the present, and the things that's coming. Know that victory has already been won, because of God's precious son!

You will be inspired and know how to acquire, access, and possess from God: and follow His instructions. After reading and listening to Lady Mary's journey of going through Hurricane Harvey and it's aftermath, you will be imparted with much information on how she, her husband, daughter, and grandchildren triumphed in all they went through.

To God be the glory!

ICU: Induced Coma Unconscious — Will You Wake Up?

This is a book that explains how we must choose to voluntarily give up the things of this world that keep us broken and bound. In giving up the things of the enemy and our flesh, we need Holy Spirit's help, and we must know what to do for ourselves. Even though we are dead to the world, we are alive in Christ Jesus.

Just like being in an Induced Coma, you are Unconscious but aware of what's going on around you. In this book you will learn how to partner with Holy Spirit and enter in. Into what you ask? The Courts of Heaven, of course, and receive from Him, and live according to His Kingdom, which is living in obedience to His Word daily.

God is simply asking, "Do you see what I (eye) see? Which eye are you looking through: The eye which has not seen, or the eye which has seen? You don't have to look far. God has allowed our lives to top the bar, right where we are!

The bed of what we see as affliction has put us in position, only with His permission. The way you enter in and go through, will determine the correct and continual outcome for you, and you will help the people around you to know what to do. Receive and obey God's Word every day, and you will receive blessings always!

Invite Christian Teacher
Lady Mary Hatter
to speak at your church or event

Lady Mary helps people walk in their purpose; which is to build up the Kingdom of God first, and then they can live effective, efficient, and excellent lives, in order to experience all that God has already promised them.

Life Coaching and Author Coaching services are also available.

Follow her on social media:

Facebook: Upe Deisgns Tsits
Twitter: @LadyMaryHatter
Instagram: upedesigns
Amazon: Click her author page and follow her

To book Lady Mary, please call
281.254.5994
or visit her website and fill out the contact form.

www.MaryHatter.com

www.ingramcontent.com/pod-product-compliance
Lightning Source LLC
Chambersburg PA
CBHW050040080526
44586CB00014B/1393